YOUR KNOWLEDGE HA

- We will publish your bachelor's and master's thesis, essays and papers

- Your own eBook and book - sold worldwide in all relevant shops

- Earn money with each sale

Upload your text at www.GRIN.com
and publish for free

Andreas Weth

Voice over IP (VoIP), a recent advance in networking technology

GRIN Verlag

Bibliografische Information der Deutschen Nationalbibliothek:

Die Deutsche Bibliothek verzeichnet diese Publikation in der Deutschen National-
bibliografie; detaillierte bibliografische Daten sind im Internet über http://dnb.d-
nb.de/ abrufbar.

Imprint:

Copyright © 2005 GRIN Verlag GmbH
Druck und Bindung: Books on Demand GmbH, Norderstedt Germany
ISBN: 978-3-638-74973-2

This book at GRIN:

http://www.grin.com/en/e-book/41861/voice-over-ip-voip-a-recent-advance-in-
networking-technology

GRIN - Your knowledge has value

Der GRIN Verlag publiziert seit 1998 wissenschaftliche Arbeiten von Studenten, Hochschullehrern und anderen Akademikern als eBook und gedrucktes Buch. Die Verlagswebsite www.grin.com ist die ideale Plattform zur Veröffentlichung von Hausarbeiten, Abschlussarbeiten, wissenschaftlichen Aufsätzen, Dissertationen und Fachbüchern.

Visit us on the internet:

http://www.grin.com/

http://www.facebook.com/grincom

http://www.twitter.com/grin_com

ISCG8036 NETWORKS AND PROTOCOLS

Semester 1, 2005

Voice over IP, a recent advance in networking technology

Assignment 2 Part Two

Andreas Christoph Weth

Wherever this assignment draws on the work of others,
such sources are clearly acknowledged.

Abbreviations

IBX   Privat Branch Exchange

IP   Internet Protocol

RTP   Real-time Transport Protocol

SDP   Session Description Protocol

SIP   Session Initiation Protocol

TCP   Transmission Control Protocol

VoIP Voice over IP

Table of Contents

1. Introduction and brief overview of Voice over IP

Voice over IP (VoIP) is at the moment one of the most discussed topics in the current network scene. Besides the theoretical interest in network development, there is always the practical relevance which is of high importance for advances in network technology. One major proof, that VoIP research and its technology has a high impact on businesses is the fact that VoIP it is already implemented in a number of companies in the United States of America, UK, Ireland and South Korea, according to Cherry (2005). The following graphic shows the importance of VoIP for companies according to a recent international study conducted by Network Computing.

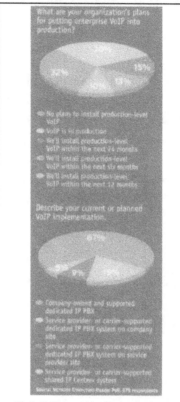

Fig.1: VoIP use and implementation survey
Source: Morrisey (2005), p.36

30% of all participants in the study confirmed a current implementation and usage
(chart 1: 30% - VoIP is in production) of VoIP technology. This indicates the high
investment activity which is currently happening in the field of VoIP. Regan
(2005) for example states that the Department of Defense (DoD) of the United
States of America established in the beginning of 2005 an over US$ 20 Mil.
contract with Nortel Networks to upgrade the current network of DoD to support
VoIP services. The main reasons for implementing VoIP are flexibility, control of
communication and cost reduction. (Regan, 2005)

To assess these benefits and to evaluate the risks of VoIP, a sound understanding
of VoIP's functionalities and principles is necessary.

3

The following report will provide the reader in the first part with an introduction and a brief overview of VoIP. In the second part of the report it is analysed how VoIP can be integrated in the current network scene and environment. Parts three and four of the essay deal with the effect of VoIP on the current technology used by organisations and the benefits resulting from VoIP. Finally in the fifth part of the report a conclusion is given to summarize the findings.

It is not easy to analyse VoIP because there isn't an industry wide definition for it. Hence, it means different things to different people. **For this research paper I will focus on the definition of VoIP as the transmission of voice over a LAN or a WAN network by using the TCP/IP protocol suite.** The transmission of voice over the public internet became also very fashionable but for complexity reasons and the reason of focusing the topic on WAN and LAN networks, I will only concentrate only on voice transmission over a WAN or LAN network and not on wireless networks. Concerning protocols, I will concentrate on the TCP/IP protocol suite and the other main standard protocols (H.323 and SIP) which are likely to become industry standards for VoIP.

However, I am a keen user of the various VoIP solutions over the public internet (which I access with a wireless LAN router) and recommend to the reader to try them out (as it is a cheap possibility of experience VoIP). Popular applications for VoIP over the public internet are in particular Skype (www.skype.com), Microsoft Netmeeting and Microsoft Messenger, Yahoo Messenger and the Apple Macinthosh iChat. There are also a number of applications available for using VoIP for UNIX and Linux platforms. (Morrissey, 2005)

The basic functionality of VoIP can be explained in a few sentences. The spoken voice gets digitized and converted into packets. Then it is transported over a network by using the Transmission Control Protocol / Internet Protocol (TCP/IP) protocol suite together with other protocols (mainly the H.323 or SIP umbrella protocols) and the sent data is reprocessed again by the receiver to hear the voice of the other person.

TCP/IP is a protocol family which covers all layers of the OSI reference model. Different layers in the OSI model are responsible for certain functionalities. For instance in the case of IP, higher layers are responsible for the retransmission and the correction of errors. In addition to that it can be said that IP is a connectionless protocol (whereas ATM for example is connection oriented). The implication of a connectionless protocol is the fact that the destination address is included in every IP packet. This means that there isn't one defined network path for all data grams. There are in most cases different network routes which can be used for data grams to arrive at the receiver. This leads to the coordination problem of these data grams as they may appear in different order at the receiver. I will focus later on the problem of managing network paths for data packages in circuit switched and packet switched networks. The coordination and management of these data grams is realized by other OSI layers.

Nevertheless, a pure IP protocol is no longer used in most VoIP implementations. Other more efficient and secure protocols were developed; also with an improvement of quality of service in mind.

According to Kuhn, Walsh & Fries (2005), the two leading protocol architectures and families which are used for most VoIP implementations are **H.323** and **SIP**. However, according to Wikipedia Encyclopedia's entry for SIP retrieved on 16 May, 2005, SIP will become the leading standard for VoIP. Experts in the field of VoIP characterise the main benefits of SIP over H.323 in its simpler architecture. (Kuhn, Walsh & Fries, 2005) Due to the fact that H.323 is already used in a high number of VoIP implementations, I will also explain the basic principles of H.323.

H.323 was originally developed for multimedia communication and its standard and architecture is managed by the International Telecommunication Union (ITU). (Mitchell, 2005) It can be seen as a standard including several other protocols, e.g. H.225 and H.245. (Kuhn, Walsh & Fries, 2005)
The main functionalities which are realised by the use of H.323 and the underlying protocols are initializing and ending voice calls as well as forwarding them. (Mitchell, 2005)
The following illustration shows how a voice call is setup with H.323 with an underlying TCP network connection.

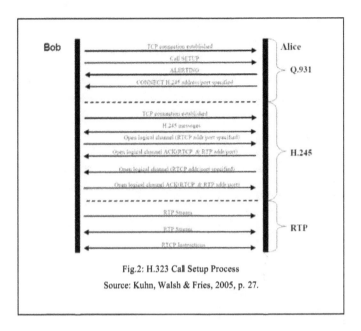

Fig.2: H.323 Call Setup Process
Source: Kuhn, Walsh & Fries, 2005, p. 27.

It would be too complex for this report to analyze all H.323 related protocols and their functionalities. However, regarding the basic parts of H.323 (which are illustrated in bold on the right side of the illustration: Q. 931, H.245 and RTP) it can be said that Q.931 mainly enables the setting up and ending of connections. In addition to that, H.245 is mainly responsible for managing the logical channels and establishing a suitable codec for the audio transmission and general logical channelling. Finally RTP stands for Real-time Transport Protocol and sets the standard for audio or video packets.

SIP (included in the TCP/IP protocol family) is a text based protocol, stands for **Session Initiation Protocol** and also uses functionalities of a number of other protocols and protocol families. SIP for instance makes use of the Real-time Transport Protocol (RTP) and the Session Description Protocol (SDP). An interesting difference compared with H.323 is the fact that SIP and its standards are managed by the Internet Engineering Task Force (IETF) whereas H.323 is managed by the International Telecommunication Union (as described above). Generally, as the name suggests, SIP is the major protocol on the internet for the initiation and the set up of sessions and works as a peer-to-peer protocol. A very application of SIP for instance is the Microsoft Messenger. These functionalities

6

are also used for its application in VoIP for managing calls and signalling transmissions. Over the network it can be carried with TCP and has many similarities compared with HTTP. (Kuhn, Walsh, Fries, 2005) The following illustration shows the basic principles of the conversation between Bob and Alice (which was already used as an example for the practical explanation of a call setup with H.323).

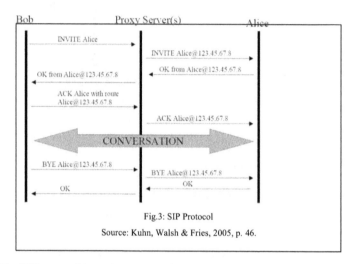

Fig.3: SIP Protocol
Source: Kuhn, Walsh & Fries, 2005, p. 46.

The SDP protocol is used to manage the communication details for initiating the call. Bob sends an invite to Alice and if she wants to answer the call, she sends a confirmation also using the SDP protocol. If the ACK (a packet which is transmitted to check the availability of TCP's services) is successful, the call can now be realised on the agreed ports and ended after the conversation.

The basic principle behind SIP is the TCP based three way handshake method which can be clearly seen in the illustration above. (Kuhn, Walsh & Fries, 2005)

After analyzing the basic protocol families used for VoIP, I will now focus on VoIP's implementation, infrastructure and interoperability issues.

The most popular applications at the moment for VoIP are IP soft phones. (Kuhn, 2005) They are realized with a computer application which performs the described tasks above by using the speakers and a microphone of a computer. Every feature of the VoIP call (dialling, storing numbers establishing the connection etc) is realized by the software. Voice digitization and the conversion into packets are also realized with the VoIP software solution. Traditional telephone calls are realized by using 64 kilobits per second for one phone call on one line, hence the good quality. Cherry (2005) states that cell phones sometimes use in a very bad connection (you are hardly able to understand the other person) a bandwidth of 10 to 15 kilobits per second. This is perfectly reasonable when you compare this reduced voice transmission quality of 10 to 15 kilobits per second with the excellent quality in a traditional circuit switched phone connection with 64 kilobits per second. The required bandwidth for VoIP or any other voice based conversation is at least 40 kilobits per second. As a comparison, it can be stated that an average small university network offers around 100 Megabits per second for all occurring network traffic. Besides the bandwidth, another issue is also the switching capacity of a communication system. The switching capacity of a data network can reach a speed of a Terabit-per-second. (Kuhn, 2005) If you compare this speed with the switching capacity of an average telephone network (around 100 bps which equals a capacity of handling around 15 000 phone calls in one second), the difference is more than a thousand fold. (Kuhn, 2005) This means almost all data networks are much cheaper on a bit and switching basis compared with telephone networks. (Kuhn, 2005)

The transmitted quality of voice is one of the most critical issues for VoIP. If the transmitted quality of voice is not sufficient, the application can not be used properly. The reader can imagine an important business phone call in which suddenly the quality of the voice transmission is suddenly reduced significantly. This explains the quality of transmission as one of the main important factors determining the success of VoIP. A sudden reduction in available bandwidth for VoIP is in most cases the major influence on the quality of transmission. The technical explanation behind this is that in most cases data packets are directly dropped if there is not enough bandwidth which leads to silence and/or missing parts of the transmission. However, Cherry (2005) thinks that bandwidth isn't a very important topic anymore as most networks offer a bandwidth which is much higher then the bandwidth necessary for VoIP. This is in my opinion a very general assumption and it always depends on the individual network together with the network and traffic management. Especially traffic priority schemes (as offered by Cisco and most other major vendors of network equipment) offer possibilities of managing enough bandwidth for voice or video services. However, Kuhn (2005) states that that the sudden increase in bandwidth in most networks caused by a boost in data transmission (think about how the size of a simple one page Microsoft Word document increased during the last ten releases of Microsoft Word) enables voice data in most cases to use overcapacity in bandwidth. The only problem is that during peak times, the network traffic needs to be managed in a way that it does not limit voice transmissions.

Besides bandwidth, other major influences on the quality of voice transmission are distortions or noises which can reduce the transmitted quality of voice.

Cherry (2005) states, that for VoIP the two main problem areas can be found in the areas of latency and hiccups. The usual cause for latency in the field of VoIP is resulting from the situation that packets are not delivered on time but arrive with a delay. Another cause is a possible deviation in the delay of packets which is called jitter. A third cause is the fact that the network eliminates packets which arrive outside of a certain time frame. According to Cherry (2005), the phenomena of latency and packet loss can lead to brief silences during the conversation. Delays generally cause echoes and various other disturbing sound effects. In comparison with latency and packet loss, hiccups are in most cases not the most difficult problem for VoIP. One directional streaming applications can be based on buffers (which can be used if there is a problem on the network). (Cherry, 2005) However, it is not possible to buffer a two directional real time VoIP call. The only solution to problems related to bandwidth is dedicating the necessary bandwidth to VoIP. This can be managed with priority management of the network traffic. Cisco for example uses a technology called Resource Reservation Protocol (RSVP) but there are various other solutions for managing bandwidth for voice transmissions. Cherry (2005) states that usually VoIP services for big companies are managed by professional telecommunication companies like AT&T. Therefore their network is designed this to have more than enough bandwidth to transport the average voice and video data. Cherry (2005) defines this network traffic management approach as over provisioning which is the standard approach for most telecommunication companies and large company networks. Nevertheless, he also states that most professional telecommunication companies have still have problems of providing voice services during peak times like Mother's day.

2. Integration of Voice over IP in current networks of organisations and in the current networking scene

This chapter of the report deals with issues about the integration of VoIP. I will first focus on the **integration of VoIP in current networks** and will evaluate **security issues** which are caused by most implementations of VoIP. After that I will analyze how **VoIP is related** to **other trends** or **developments in the networking scene** and how VoIP could influence this scene.

As it is already included in its definition, VoIP uses a TCP network for the transmission of voice data. It is also possible to use other protocols and protocol families like Framerelay or ATM for these services. However, in the case of VoIP the TCP/IP protocol suit is used – as already described above – to transport and connect the speakers. As long as VoIP is realised in a closed network and no existing analogue or digital phones are connected, no devices for converting voice to IP are needed besides the IP soft phone. However, if an ordinary analogue or digital phone is connected to this network, there are several implementation possibilities which are shown in the following graphic.

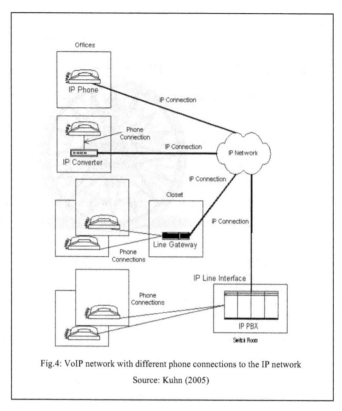

Fig.4: VoIP network with different phone connections to the IP network

Source: Kuhn (2005)

Either an IP converter, a line gateway or an IP line interface can be used for connecting standard telephones (based on circuit switching) to the IP network hence enabling VoIP. A converter, gateway or interface are necessary because IP (hence VoIP) is based on packet switching technology (which can be also called cell switching technology) which is illustrated in the following figure.

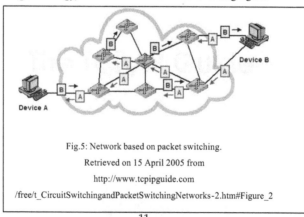

Fig.5: Network based on packet switching.

Retrieved on 15 April 2005 from

http://www.tcpipguide.com

/free/t_CircuitSwitchingandPacketSwitchingNetworks-2.htm#Figure_2

A standard telephone can not be directly connected to an IP network because public telephone networks are based on circuit switching technology which is illustrated in the following illustration.

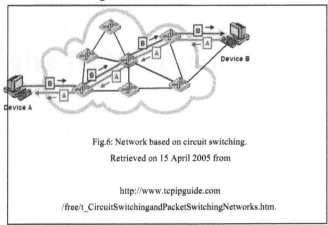

Fig.6: Network based on circuit switching.
Retrieved on 15 April 2005 from

http://www.tcpipguide.com
/free/t_CircuitSwitchingandPacketSwitchingNetworks.htm.

Circuit switching means electric circuits between two phones are switched to use a whole channel for the voice transmission.

If you compare the two illustrations above, it becomes clear that in a network based on circuit switching (Figure 6) all packets (As) travel the same way to the receiver and in case of a network based on packet switching, packets can travel a different way (which can be seen if you compare the routes of the As in Figure 5). Unfortunately there is no direct interoperability between circuit and packet switching technology without further use of technology (converters, gateways or interfaces) due to a number of reasons. One reason for example is the fact that over a packet switched network data is processed and converted into frames and packets with variable sizes.

After clarifying the basic technological functionalities of VoIP networks, I will now focus on security issues of VoIP.

Concerning security issues resulting from the implementation of VoIP, it must be said that a high amount of new security threats come up with the implementation of VoIP. (Rendon, 2004) Securing the network alone does not mean security concerning VoIP is also covered. (Rendon, 2004) Probably the most important

12

publication about security in VoIP networks is the study Security Considerations for Voice over IP Systems from Kuhn, Walsh & Fries (2005) published by the National Institute of Standards and Technology & Department of Commerce United States of America. As it is well known that intelligence services from the USA developed a number of possibilities of intercepting VoIP and other communications, it seems that the study was made from the leading experts in this field.

Kuhn, Walsh & Fries (2005) describe firewalls as the most important issue to secure a VoIP network. The only problem resulting from the implementation of a firewall is the fact that they do not prevent protection from internal hackers. In addition to that, firewalls and intrusion protection systems must be configured or the use of VoIP. Otherwise they do not provide adequate security for the network (Kuhn, Walsh & Fries, 2005). However, I will analyse other security measures besides firewalls and intrusion protection.

The two other main options for implementing internal security in a VoIP network are tunnelling and encryption. When SIP is used, IPsec is an efficient way to protect the SIP hosts and the traffic in the network with the use of tunnelling and encryption. (Kuhn, Walsh & Fries, 2005) The basic principle of IPsec is the fact that the header and the load of the packages are encrypted in the tunnel mode of IPsec. (Kuhn, Walsh & Fries, 2005) When an intruder now receives a package sent over the network, he is not able to process the information of the header and the content of the packet. (Kuhn, Walsh & Fries, 2005) In addition to that, HTTP authentification can be used to prevent intruders.

According to Kuhn, Walsh & Fries (2005), encryption can cause an expansion in packet size (which leads to higher traffic on the network) and increased latency which places high demands on the chosen encryption standard.

The other main measure of increasing security when VoIP is used is appropriate network architecture. Different subnets and separate DHCP servers can increase the shelter of implemented intrusion protection and firewalls. (Kuhn, Walsh & Fries, 2005)

Finally, Kuhn, Walsh & Fries (2005) state that also physical access to network equipments and VoIP client computers should be secured as even with appropriate encryption, traffic analysis can be conducted by intruders (e.g. it can be found out who communicates with whom etc).

13

After the analysis of security issues for VoIP, I focus now on the other fields of the current networking scene which are related to VoIP.

VoIP is related to several other trends in the networking scene. Video transmission is another trend which is related to VoIP. Video and Audio real time transmissions have the hightest requirements on a network and its configuration. For managing video transmissions over a company network, a very high dedicated bandwidth is necessary. As with VoIP, a suitable system for network traffic priority management and dedicating bandwidth to video streaming packets is necessary. Real time two way video transmission deals with almost identical problems compared with VoIP. Therefore the research which is done for the reduction of distortion, delays, latency, packet loss and hiccups is highly relevant for VoIP as well as for video and other real time two way (but also one way) transmissions over a packet switched network. I excluded VoIP in wireless networks but in these networks, it will be even more difficult to manage the necessary bandwidth for VoIP. However, existing mobile networks show that voice transmission is possible in wireless environments even for huge networks with a large number of clients and gigantic differences between the average and peak time load of the network.

The other main research field with which VoIP is related are protocols. VoIP is related to so many protocols it does not make sense to state every protocol which is used for VoIP services. However, the main protocol families are TCP, H.323 and ISP which were already analysed in previous chapters.

Other research fields of the current networking scene which are related to VoIP are network software and equipment; mainly routers, gateways and switches but also servers, server software and physical network connections (especially development in fiber but also in satellite communication).

The last and most general field which VoIP is related to is network architecture and particular development in the field of IP LAN or WAN networks. As this form of networks which is mainly based on the TCP/IP protocol suite is already very popular for many companies and especially the internet, it can be said that heavy development will happen in this field in the next years.

3. The effect of Voice over IP on the current technology used by organisations

After explaining the other fields in the current networking scene which are related to VoIP, I will focus now on implications of VoIP for the current used technology of organisations. Most experts in the field of networks and telecommunication are sure that companies will definitely switch to VoIP sooner or later. Therefore the primary effect of that development is that existing telephone networks will become obsolete. Investments into traditional telephone networks are therefore no longer reasonable, according to most experts in the field of networks and telecommunication. Probably most companies will keep a few circuit switched telephone lines (or maybe mobile phones as this technology is more mature and usually offers a very good quality of service in most major cities, compared with a early VoIP implementations) for emergency issues or very important conversations. However, as the increase in traffic resulting from the use of VoIP telephony will augment, the requirement on the network equipment will also increase significantly. There will be problems with traditional copper lines as these networks won't be able to provide the necessary bandwidth for big companies. However, a high number of companies already implemented fiber lines which provide more than enough capacity for most VoIP applications.

Other effects of VoIP on the current technology of organisations will be found in the fields of protocols, network infrastructure and network equipment. It depends on the particular VoIP system which network requirements there are; especially routers, router software, protocols (for instance IPv6 instead of IPv4) or server equipment are likely to be changed when a VoIP system is implemented.

4. Critical examination of the benefits of Voice over IP for organisations

It is impossible to analyse and quantify the exact benefits of average VoIP implementations because the benefits depend on a number of factors and on the individual implementation. However, I will state the main benefits and the fields where these factors can be realized.

Cost reduction is the main argument which is used by the leading vendors of VoIP applications and equipment. There is in most cases an initial investment necessary in VoIP technology which is mainly related to investments in network architecture (lines, network equipment and necessary upgrades from network equipment). However, cost reductions resulting from the use of VoIP are in most cases significantly higher than initial investments in network architecture.

Cost reduction benefits result from the following factors:

- **Reduction in running costs** (especially long distance phone calls and leasing fees for telephone equipment),
- **Reduced investment in new communication equipment** (most employees are already working with PCs which are capable of VoIP, hence there is not longer a need for buying telephones or telephone switching equipment. In most cases a head set for US$ 10 is sufficient for VoIP telephone.),
- **Reduced maintenance and service costs** (the maintenance and the service of VoIP can be provided in most cases by the IT department. There is no longer a need for extensive maintenance of the corporate telephone network by external companies.).

Therefore the popularity of VoIP will result in a decrease in costs of communication for most companies and also in a revenue reduction of traditional phone companies. However, Cherry (2005) states that many phone companies already use VoIP or other data networks for transferring voice data on longer distances but do not pass this cost advantage to the customer.

Increased efficiency for many employees is another main argument which can be stated for the use of VoIP. Various solutions are able to provide an all in one application for email, fax, VoIP, chat clients and other communication tools. This means the user can for example use the same contact database to write emails, make phone calls, chat and include important business information. Currently, most companies have different systems for different communication needs running at the same time, e.g. Outlook, Skype, MSN messenger etc. These functionalities will be provided in the near future by one software solution and will lead to a higher efficiency of employees because it will be easier for them to communicate with one solution. According to Cherry (2005), simplification leads also to efficiency benefits. He thinks that an integrated data and voice network leads to standardization.

Flexibility is the next important benefit resulting from a VoIP implementation. (Black, 2002) There is no longer a need for telephone networks to communicate. By using LAN connections and the IP network, employees will be able to telephone at any place where a suitable LAN connection is provided.

The last identified argument for the use of VoIP can be found in the field of **multi service and multimedia application architecture.** (Cherry, 2005) Most current telephone systems are not able to provide the services which are requested by current multi service applications. Many enterprise resource planning systems (e.g. SAP) are based on a services oriented architecture. Some features can only be realized with a VoIP implementation. According to Cherry (2005), will the number of multi service applications rise in the near future. Hence, there will be a need for VoIP services and infrastructure.

5. Conclusion and Summary

The research report gave a basic introduction to VoIP's commonly used protocols, architecture and security features.
VoIP can be integrated into the current network of companies with the use of **bandwidth and traffic priority management.** H.323 and SIP are the most common protocol families which are used for VoIP implementations. Traditional **analogue phones** or **circuit switched telephone networks** can be connected to a VoIP network by using an **IP converter, a line gateway** or an **IP line interface** which shows the interoperability of VoIP networks with traditional circuit switched telephone networks. In addition to that, different possibilities of **securing VoIP transmissions** were briefly analyzed, mainly in the field of **network architecture** together with **external network measures (firewalls)** but also **internal security measures (encryption and tunnelling).** The main fields for the **impact of VoIP** of the **current networking scene** were identified: mainly **protocols, network equipment and network architecture.** Also the **substitution of circuit switched telephone networks** was identified as one of the major **impact** of VoIP on the **technology of organisations.** Finally, the **main benefits of VoIP** for organisations were analyzed and located in the areas of **cost**

reduction, employee efficiency, flexibility and multi service / multimedia application architecture.

Concerning the future development of VoIP, the next major developments will be definitely happen in the area of wireless access and connectivity of mobile devices to VoIP networks. All major Cell phone producers are experimenting at the moment with mobile phones which are capable of both wireless VoIP and and third generation (3G) mobile network accessibility.

Besides all positive aspects of VoIP, Cherry (2005) thinks that VoIP can not totally replace regular telephone networks in the next few years. Quality of service is still not sufficient during peak times so regular telephone networks well continue to exist in the next years. However, technical developments usually went faster as even the experts predicted so it will be very interesting when VoIP together with networks for mobile telephony will completely replace current circuit switched telephone networks.

References

Black, U. (2002). **Voice Over IP (2nd Edition)**. New Jersey: Prentice Hall.

Cherry, S. (2005). **Seven Myths about Voice over IP**. Retrieved on 14 April, 2005 from
http://www.spectrum.ieee.org/WEBONLY/publicfeature/mar05/0305vip.html.

Denes, Shary (2005). VoIP in 2005. **Rural Telecommunications**, Mar/Apr2005, Vol. 24 Issue 2, p8.

Kuhn, R., Walsh, T. & Fries, S. (2005). **Security Considerations for Voice over IP Systems.** Gaithersburg: National Institute of Standards and Technology & Department of Commerce United States of America.

Kuhn, R. (2005). **UNDERSTANDING VOICE OVER IP**. Retrieved on 8 April, 2005 from http://www.compassconsulting.com/articles/voipintro.html.

Mitchell, B. (2005). **H.323 Protocol**. Retrieved on 14 April, 2005 from http://compnetworking.about.com/cs/voicefaxoverip/g/bldef_h323.htm.

Morissey, P. (2005). VoIP: JOIN THE PARTY. **Network Computing**, 3/17/2005, Vol. 16 Issue 5, 32 – 36.

Regan, K. (2005). **Defense Department Adopts VoIP Technology**. Retrieved on 14 April, 2005 from http://www.ecommercetimes.com/rsstory/41914.html.

Rendon, Jim (2004). **The security risks of VoIP**. Retrieved on 10 April, 2005 from
http://searchcio.techtarget.com/originalContent/0,289142,sid19_gci1032194,00.html.